FINDING OUT ABOUT

TRUCKS

by
ARTHUR W. TIMMS

ENSLOW PUBLISHERS
Bloy Street and Ramsey Avenue
Box 777
Hillside, NJ 07205

Finding-Out Books

Library of Congress Cataloging in Publication Data:

Timms, Arthur W.
    Finding out about trucks.
    (Finding-out books)

    SUMMARY: Describes and illustrates many varieties
of trucks and how they function.
    1. Motor-trucks–Juvenile literature. [1. Trucks]
I. Title.

TL230.T53   629.2'24   80-14559
ISBN 0-89490-037-4 (lib.bdg.)

Printed in the United States of America

10 9 8 7 6 5 4 3 2

FINDING OUT ABOUT TRUCKS

Everyone likes trucks. This is a book about the many kinds of trucks, the many features special to trucks, and the trucking industry. Let's define a truck as a vehicle that moves a load (commodity) from one point (origination point) to another point (destination point).

Trucks come in many sizes and shapes.

All trucks, in order to move, must have wheels. The wheels go on each end of the axle. Axles may have SINGLE TIRES or DUAL TIRES.

Single-Tired Wheels

Dual-Tired Wheels

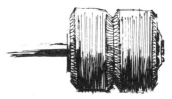

Trucks are grouped according to the number of axles they have. A truck may be a SINGLE-AXLE TRUCK,which really means it has one drive axle and one steering axle.

Single-Axle Truck

A TANDEM-AXLE TRUCK has two drive axles and one steering axle.

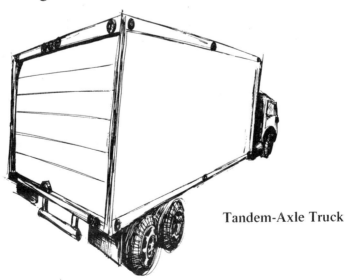

Tandem-Axle Truck

Trucks are also grouped according to the type of frame they have. If the engine, cab, and body (commodity area) are all on the same frame, the truck is called a STRAIGHT TRUCK.

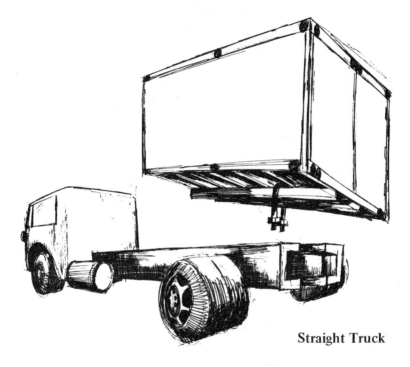

Straight Truck

If the engine and cab are separate from the body, the truck is called a TRACTOR-TRAILER COMBINATION. The cab and engine are in a unit called the tractor, and the body, called the trailer, is joined to the tractor.

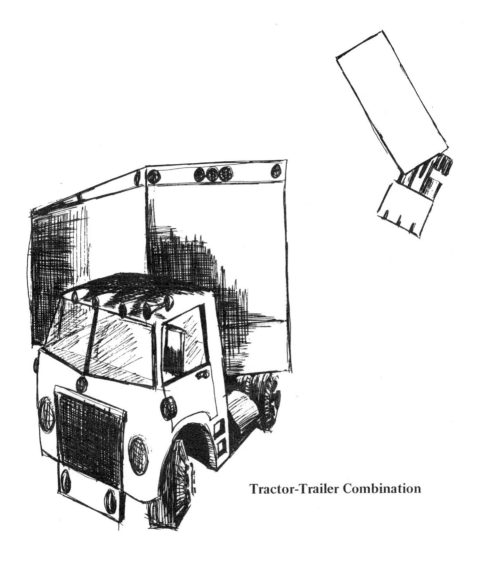

Tractor-Trailer Combination

A trailer must have a tractor under it to give it a front set of wheels. This trailer unit is called a SEMI-TRAILER.

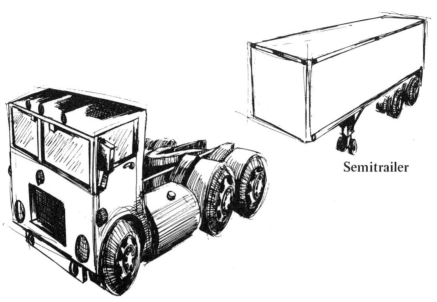

Semitrailer

The trailer is connected to the tractor by means of a
FIFTH WHEEL. This fifth wheel is mounted on the
rear of the tractor. It does several very important
things. It keeps the tractor and trailer in proper
positions, it allows for sliding at the swivel area, and
it is where the trailer locks to the tractor.

Under the front of the trailer there is a KINGPIN.
The kingpin slides into the fifth wheel and forms a
swivel connection. This swivel connection makes it
easier to move big, heavy loads.

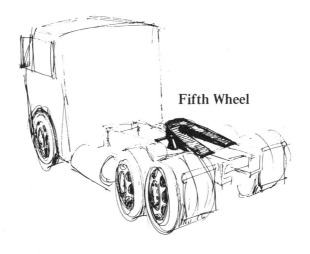

Fifth Wheel

The bottom of the trailer over the kingpin is made of heavy-duty steel. This area of the trailer is called the UPPER-COUPLER AREA.

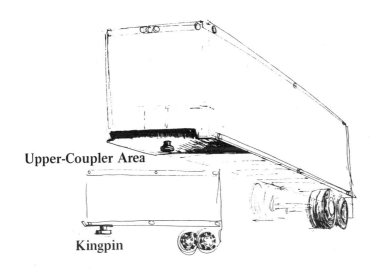

Upper-Coupler Area

Kingpin

11

If you were to look at a tractor without the trailer attached, you would see that the fifth wheel is covered with heavy grease. The grease is put there on purpose so that the tractor and trailer will swivel easily.

Trailers, just as trucks, are grouped as single-axle or tandem-axle trailers.

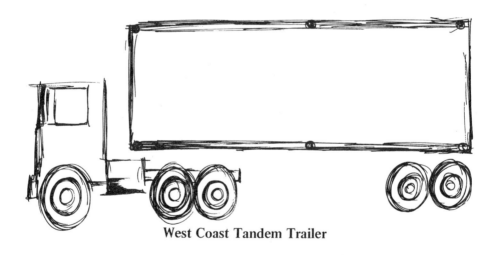

West Coast Tandem Trailer

The WEST COAST TANDEM TRAILER has the axles at the rear of the trailer.

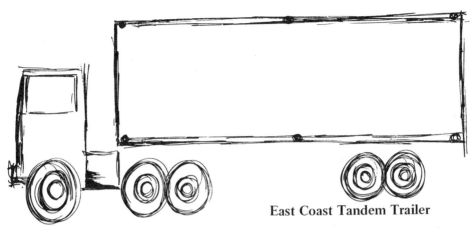

East Coast Tandem Trailer

The EAST COAST TANDEM TRAILER has the axles under the trailer and gives more flexibility in tight spaces. The two axles of the tandem can be spread apart as much as nine feet. When the axles are spread it becomes a SPREAD-AXLE TRAILER. It can take more weight since the weight is distributed over a wider axle area.

Spread-Axle Trailer

The CATERPILLAR TRAILER has even more axles to carry more weight.

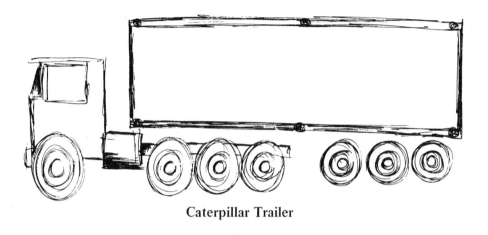

Caterpillar Trailer

The number of axles, the number of wheels, and the general shape of any truck are determined by the weight of the load it will carry. The more weight it will carry, the more axles, wheels, and length the truck will have. If the weight of a load is spread over a larger area, there is more braking power and less damage to the surface of the road.

Truck manufacturers and government regulations have put limits on load sizes and truck lengths. The limit that can be carried by a truck of a certain length is called the truck's G.V.W. or GROSS VEHICLE WEIGHT.

Since the weight of a load must be shared by each of the axles, trucks whose G.V.W. is great may have more than the basic single-axle/tandem-axle set-up.

For very heavy or large loads two trailers may be used with one tractor. This arrangement is called a SET OF DOUBLES or DOUBLE BOTTOMS.

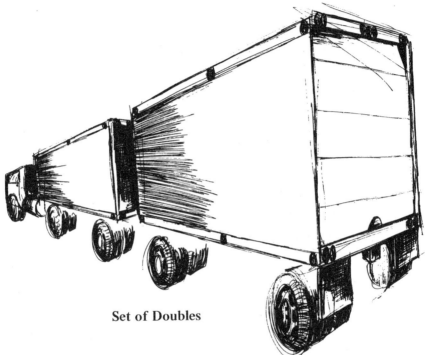

Set of Doubles

There are TRI-AXLE TRUCKS and TRI-AXLE TRAILERS.

A third axle can be attached to the rear of a tractor to make a single-axle tractor into a tandem-axle tractor. This added axle does not help with the driving. It simply "tags along," and so is called a TAG AXLE.

Tri-Axle Truck

Tri-Axle Trailer

17

Some tag axles can be lifted by air pressure when not in use. This kind of axle is called a LIFTING TAG AXLE.

Tag Axle

Lifting Tag Axle

Trucks are sometimes grouped according to where the engine is located. If the engine is in the front of the driver's section, the truck is called a CONVENTIONAL TRUCK.

Conventional Truck

If the engine is placed under the driver's section, the truck is called a CAB-OVER-ENGINE or C.O.E. TRUCK. Longer trailers can be used with this type of truck.

Cab-Over-Engine Truck

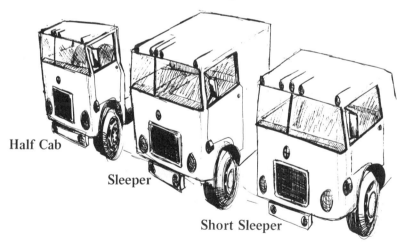

Half Cab

Sleeper

Short Sleeper

There are three types of C.O.E.'s. The HALF CAB type is used to pull a trailer of maximum length.

The SLEEPER is wider than the half cab by the width of a full mattress. Sleepers are used on long, non-stop trips when the truck must keep moving at all times. There are usually two drivers on these non-stop trips, who work together as a team. One sleeps while the other drives. Drivers may also want to use the sleeper while the truck is being loaded or unloaded, or if they arrive at their destination early.

The SHORT SLEEPER, or THREE-QUARTER SLEEPER allows for narrower mattresses and slightly longer trailers.

Everything we use moves, at some point, in a truck. Raw materials are moved to the manufacturer by truck. Finished or processed materials are moved by truck from the manufacturer to the stores where we buy them.

Special trucks have been designed to move special types of loads.

Dry goods are commodities that usually come in packages. They need no special care other than being kept dry. This kind of load is carried in a VAN.

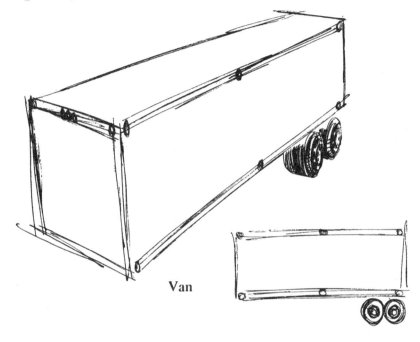

Van

Perishable goods sometimes must be kept hot or cold, depending on the outside temperature, so that they will not spoil. The truck designed to move this kind of load is called a REEFER, or REFRIGERATED VAN. It is called a refrigerated van even though it can keep things hot as well as cold. Its ceiling, floor, and walls are insulated.

The reefer has its own temperature-control unit. This unit is self-contained, and can either heat or cool. It is called a refrigeration unit.

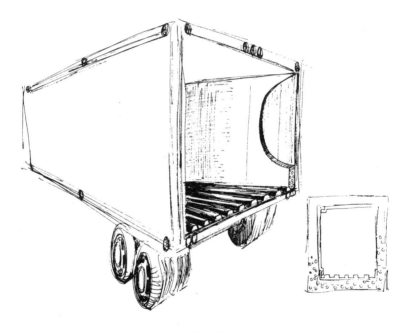

Reefer

The refrigeration unit can be placed on the front (nose) of the trailer and is then called a NOSEMOUNT UNIT.

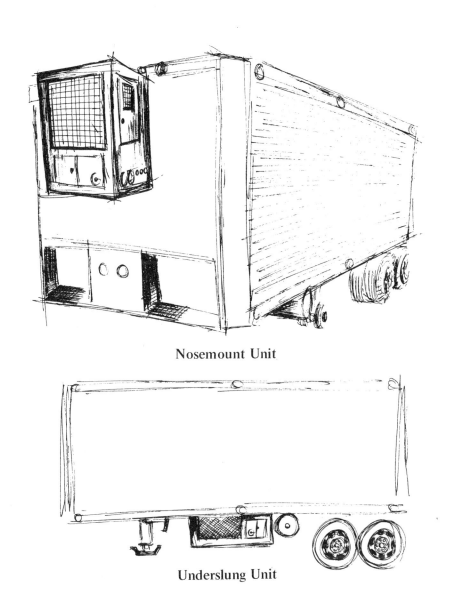

Nosemount Unit

Underslung Unit

It also can be placed under the trailer and is called an
UNDERSLUNG UNIT, or an UNDERMOUNT.

There is a special kind of refrigerated van used to carry meat. It is a reefer with rails on the ceiling where the meat is hung. This van is called a RAILER. When meat is carried this way it never touches the floor.

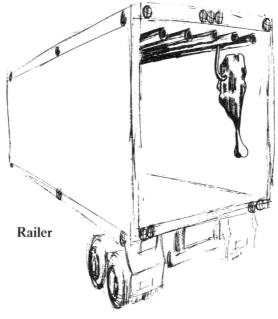

Railer

Some meat-carrying vans are equipped with a TRACK SYSTEM. The tracks in the ceiling of the trailer are connected to tracks in the ceiling of the meat-packing plant by an extension piece. As the meat is prepared at the plant it is placed on HANGERS. The hangers have wheels that roll the meat along the tracks and right into the truck. Meat loaded this way stays clean because it never touches the floor.

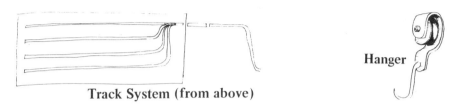

Track System (from above)

Hanger

Cattle are carried to the meat processor in a LIVESTOCK VAN. Since the cattle must arrive at the meat-processing plant alive, the livestock van has many holes in it so that the animals will have enough air to breathe.

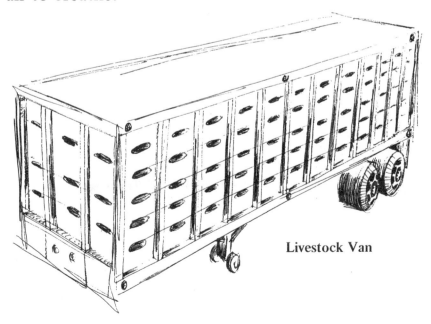

Livestock Van

The rear doors of the livestock van are sometimes made in such a way that the animals must move in single file while they are being loaded and unloaded. This prevents them from becoming bunched or injured.

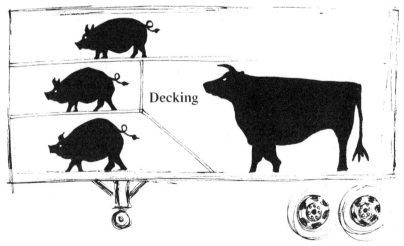

Decking

When the van is being used to carry small animals, such as pigs, it may have two or three floors in it at different levels. This permits more animals to be moved in the van on decks or by DECKING.

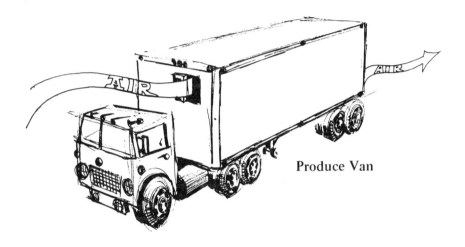

Produce Van

Sometimes vegetables are carried in a PRODUCE VAN. This van does not need as much insulation as the reefer because vegetables do not need to be kept very cold. Vegetables do need a constant flow of moist air. So the produce van has VENT DOORS. The vent doors are placed in the upper front of the trailer and in the lower rear of the trailer. Air then moves through the truck while the truck is moving.

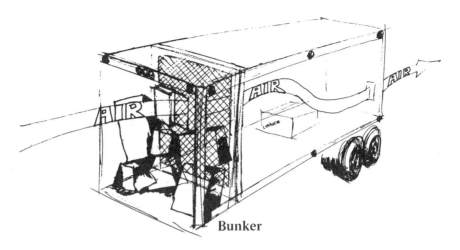
Bunker

There may also be a small compartment made out of wire in the front of the trailer. It is filled with blocks of ice that cool and moisten the air as it moves through the vent door in the front. This small compartment is called a BUNKER.

Sometimes a small fan is used to help the air flow. The fan is called a BLOWER or PUTT-PUTT. So a produce van may be set up with a BUNKER/BLOWER system.

A truck used to move furniture from one house to another is called a FURNITURE VAN, HOUSE-HOLD-GOODS VAN, OR MOVING VAN.

Furniture comes in odd sizes and shapes. Therefore the floor of the furniture van is made very close to the ground to provide a lot of space. The low frame also makes it easier to load heavy, awkward furniture because it does not have to be lifted as high. This type of frame is called a DROPFRAME.

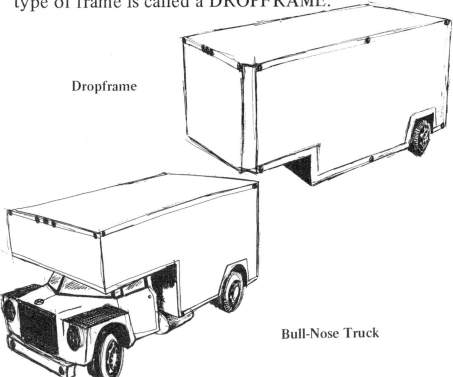

Dropframe

Bull-Nose Truck

A type of straight truck with an extension built over the cab is often used for furniture moving. The extension is referred to as a BULL NOSE or ATTIC.

Most trailers have posts that hold up the sides. Furniture vans also have posts that run from the floor to the ceiling and from the front to the back. These posts have slots and holes in them so that the movers can tie or lock pieces of furniture into place. These posts are called VERTICAL LOGISTICS POSTS if they go from floor to ceiling and HORIZONTAL LOGISTICS POSTS if they run the length of the trailer.

Electronic equipment is hauled in a special type of van called an ELECTRONICS VAN. The electronics van may not have as much room inside it as the furniture van, but it must be low, and it must have a level floor (without a wheel box at the rear of the trailer, caused by the shape of the conventional wheel/axle construction). There must be nothing to obstruct the tow motors used to load and unload the heavy equipment.

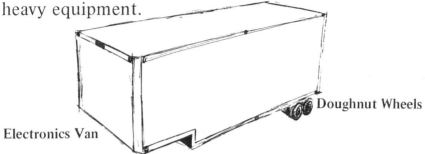

Electronics Van
Doughnut Wheels

The low, level floor is produced by using small tires called DOUGHNUT WHEELS.

The electronics van will also ride on rubber bags filled with air instead of on springs. These are called AIR BAGS. This air-ride suspension system moves equipment without jarring it because it reduces the bumps felt by the wheels and axles before they reach the truck.

Air Bags

Liquids of all kinds are moved in large drums on wheels. This type of trailer is called a TANK TRAILER.

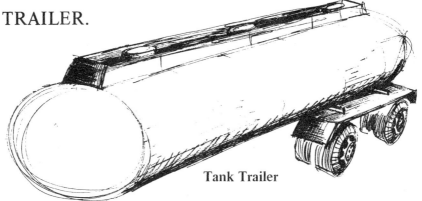

Tank Trailer

Different types of liquids require different types of tank trailers. One type of trailer has a smooth interior very much like the barrel of a gun. Strength is added to the drum by reinforcing rings on the outside. This type of trailer is called a CLEAN-BORE EXTERNAL-RING TRAILER.

Clean-Bore External-Ring Trailer

Another kind of tank trailer is made up of a series of compartments separated by walls. This type is called the INTERNAL COMPARTMENTIZED TANK. The single or double walls separating the compartments are called BULKHEADS.

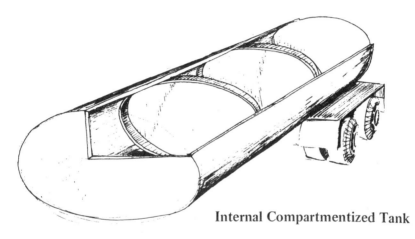

Internal Compartmentized Tank

Sometimes the bulkhead is made with a hole in the center. The hole slows down the surge or movement

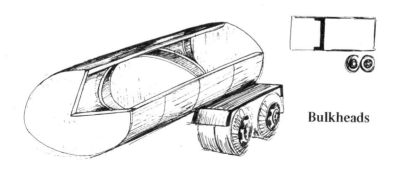

Bulkheads

of the liquid when the truck starts or stops. This kind of bulkhead is called a BAFFLE.

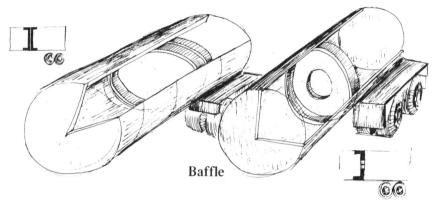

Baffle

Tank trailers that carry liquids are made of steel, aluminum, or stainless steel. Sometimes they are lined with rubber or glass.

These tank trailers have three basic shapes. The STRAIGHT FRAME has no slope. The SINGLE-CONICAL FRAME has a slope to either end. The DOUBLE-CONICAL FRAME slopes from both sides to the middle.

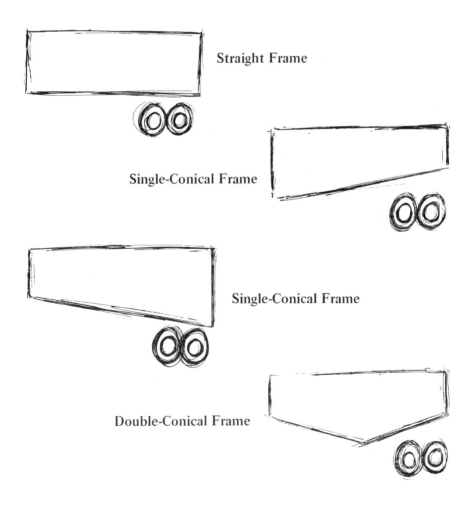

Straight Frame

Single-Conical Frame

Single-Conical Frame

Double-Conical Frame

There is a special kind of tank trailer designed to carry dry materials that are in granular or pellet form. Cements, grains, or fertilizers are carried in these DRY-BULK TRAILERS.

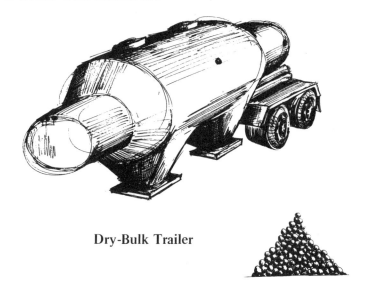

Dry-Bulk Trailer

This trailer has a pressurized air line under its sloping sides. When the valve is opened, the product slides into the air line and is directed by the air pressure to a desired place at the unloading site. The engine that supplies the air pressure can be carried on the truck or attached at the unloading site. It is called a BLOWER.

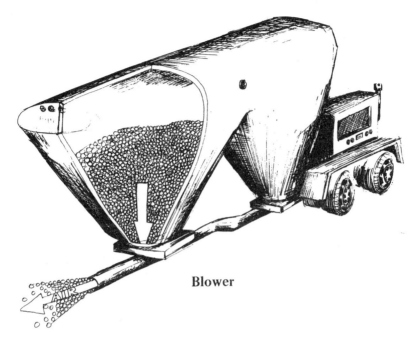

Blower

Large products such as steel or lumber that need to
be loaded by cranes are carried on a PLATFORM
TRAILER or FLATBED TRAILER.

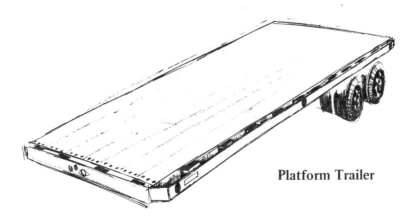

Platform Trailer

Flatbed trailers are often made to be expanded for longer loads. The expandable trailer is called a TELESCOPIC TRAILER.

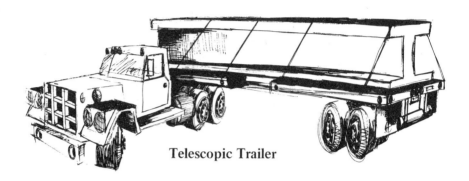

Telescopic Trailer

If more space is needed, a trailer with a platform closer to the ground can be used. This is called a DROPFRAME PLATFORM.

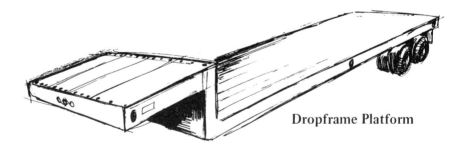

Dropframe Platform

The area where the platform (or deck) drops is called the GOOSENECK.

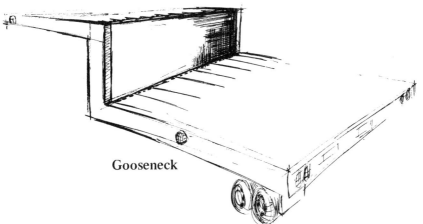

Gooseneck

Trailers designed to carry heavy machinery often have a FOLDING GOOSENECK. The trailer is unhooked from the tractor, the gooseneck folds flat to the ground, and the machinery can be driven directly off the trailer.

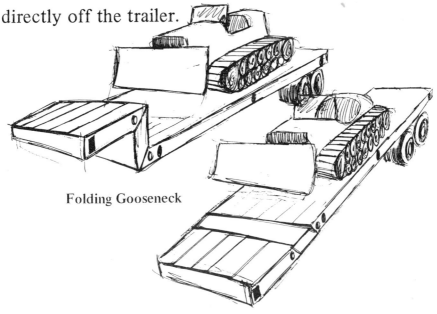

Folding Gooseneck

A REMOVABLE GOOSENECK is actually detached from the trailer but remains attached to the tractor. It can be operated by hand or by a motor. If it has a motor it is called a hydraulic gooseneck.

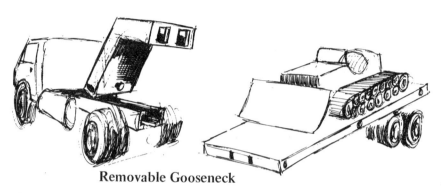

Removable Gooseneck

A very large and heavy load is carried on an even lower trailer built to handle added weight. This trailer is called a LOW BOY or DOUBLE-DROP PLATFORM.

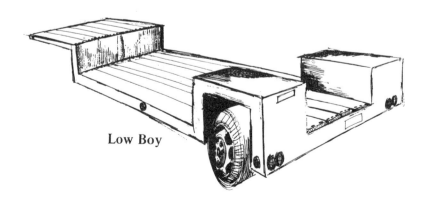

Low Boy

Many Low Boys have a slope extension at the rear. This extension is called a BEAVER TAIL. Here also the machinery can be driven directly on and off.

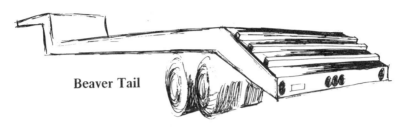

Beaver Tail

Low Boys may have extensions on the side, called outriggers, for moving over-width loads. The SWING OUTRIGGER stays against the side when it is not being used. The DRAWER-TYPE OUTRIGGER is pushed in like a drawer when it is not being used.

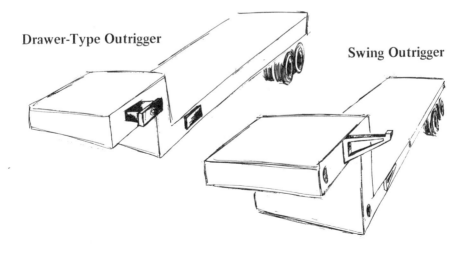

Drawer-Type Outrigger

Swing Outrigger

To avoid handling products often, they can be loaded in movable boxes called containers. Some are smaller than a normal trailer and can be stacked on board a ship. Others may be as large as a trailer. These containers have no wheels. They are lifted off a ship and placed on a set of wheels to be moved on land. The wheels and frame are called the BOGIE or CHASSIS.

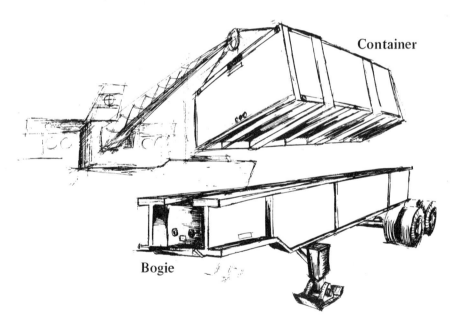

Container

Bogie

Often two small containers can be carried on the same chassis. Loaded containers can be stored on legs until a chassis returns with empty containers. This is called the SWAP-BODY SYSTEM.

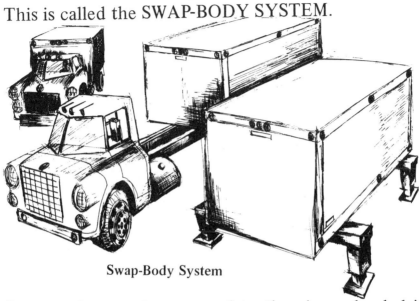

Swap-Body System

Cargoes that can be exposed to the air are hauled in DUMP TRUCKS or DUMP TRAILERS. These trucks have an open top for loading and a panel at the rear that opens for unloading when the front is raised.

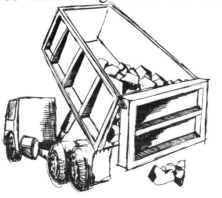

Dump Truck

The basic tractor-trailer combination has 18 wheels.

There are two basic types of wheels. The first type is a SPOKE WHEEL. This was the first type of steel truck wheel to be used and is similar to a wagon wheel. The tire and rim are mounted onto the wheel by a LUG, a STUD, and a CLAMP.

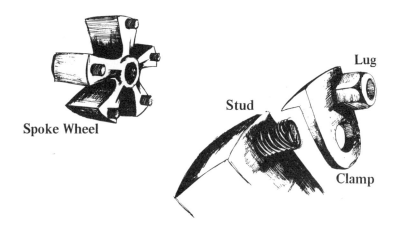

Spoke Wheel

Lug

Stud

Clamp

Most spoke wheels have five spokes. There are advantages and disadvantages to the five-spoke arrangement. When the tires need to be changed there are only five lugs to tighten or loosen. However, if the lugs are not tightened (torqued) properly, the wheel doesn't run true and can damage tires, bearings, or brakes.

Disc Wheel

The second type of wheel, called the DISC WHEEL, has ten studs but no lugs or clamps. Since the studs are tightened toward the center of the wheel when the tire is changed, the wheel runs true. Holes in the disc permit air to cool the brakes. This type of wheel works very well in high-speed and mountain driving where brakes are used often.

Saving fuel is very important to the trucking industry. When the wind hits the frontal area of a heavy trailer directly, it forces the tractor pulling it to use more fuel. Wind currents can be forced over the top of the trailer by placing a WIND DEFLECTOR, or AIR FOIL, on the tractor. This way less fuel is needed to pull the trailer.

Air Foil

Another way of deflecting the wind currents and saving fuel is by placing a NOSE CONE, made of fiberglass, on the trailer.

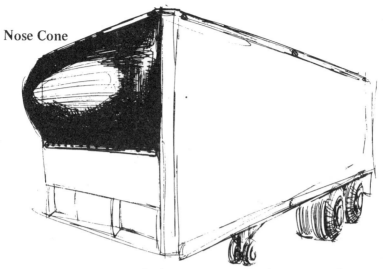

Nose Cone

Different types of doors are used on trucks carrying different types of cargo. The most common type of door, called the FULL-OPENING DOOR, or SWING DOOR, is in the rear of the truck. These doors give a very wide opening for loading or unloading large cargo.

Full-Opening Door

Overhead Door

Like the door of many garages, the OVERHEAD DOOR, or ROLL-UP DOOR, of a truck rolls into the top of the trailer. This type of door saves both time and labor. The driver can back directly to a loading dock and open the door. He does not need space or time to get out of the truck, swing the full-opening doors open, get back in, and back closer to the dock.

Sometimes the loading or unloading area is too small to permit a truck to be backed into it. Then the truck must have SIDE DOORS that open either on the road side or the curb side. This type of door also permits the driver to unload cargo that has been placed in the front or middle of the truck.

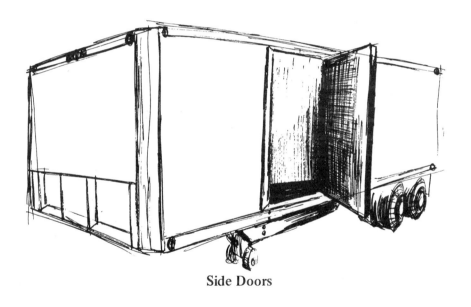

Side Doors

Some trucks carry extra loading space in a box between the tractor and trailer. This extra box is called a DROMEDARY. The dromedary can carry small cargo, ready to be delivered while the large trailer is being unloaded. It also can be insulated to carry refrigerated goods when the large trailer has no insulation. Can you think of other uses for the dromedary?

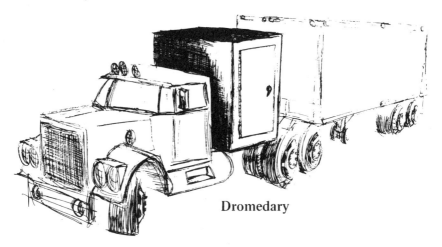

Dromedary

There are certain pieces of equipment that can change the weight distribution of a truck for long, light, or heavy loads. The SLIDING TANDEM (or SLIDER) is a running gear mounted on the slide rails at the rear of the trailer. A bar or pin locks the running gear into the particular hole location needed.

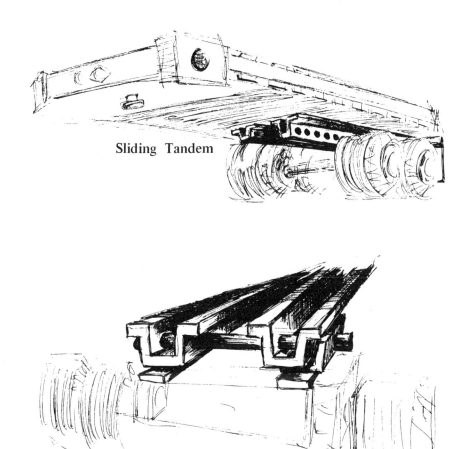

Sliding Tandem

Like the sliding tandem, a SLIDING FIFTH WHEEL
is used to change weight distribution. The sliding
fifth wheel, mounted on the tractor, moves forward
or backward, putting the trailer closer to or farther
from the tractor. Both the sliding fifth wheel and the

sliding tandem can be moved by hand or adapted to be moved by air pressure.

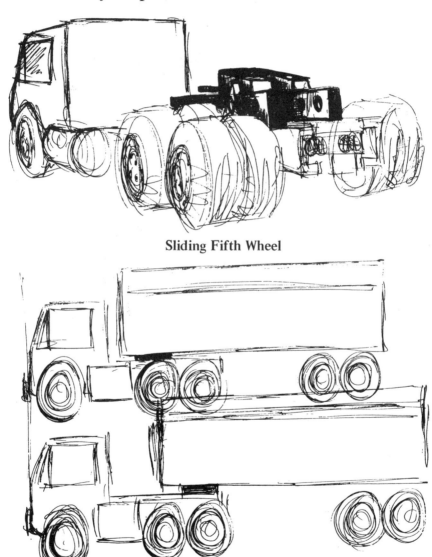

Sliding Fifth Wheel

Most tractors travel an average of only five miles on a gallon of fuel. Imagine how much fuel is needed to travel 3,000 miles! Even though FUEL TANKS, made of aluminum or steel and carried on the side of a tractor can store extra fuel, the driver also must stop at truck stops for fuel.

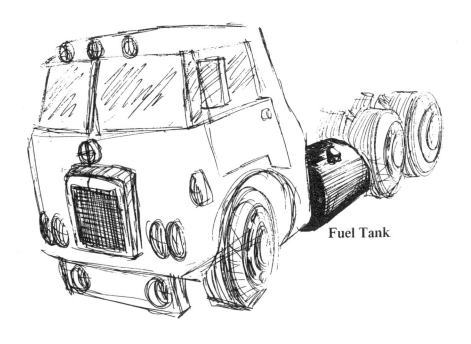

Fuel Tank

The grill on the front of the truck often has SHUTTERS that are set to open automatically, allowing air to cool a hot engine, or to close, keeping the heat in to warm a cold engine.

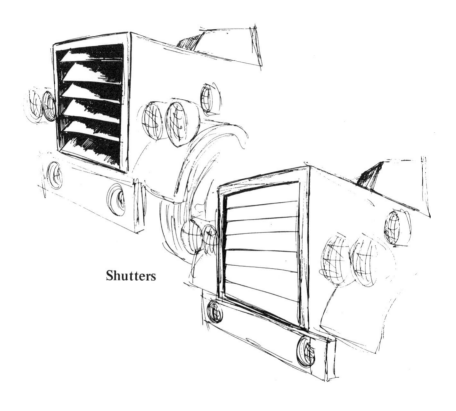

Shutters

A BUG SCREEN, placed over the grill, protects the engine from bugs—and curious fingers! The shutters may open or close even when the truck isn't moving. You must remember never to touch the grill of a truck. Your fingers could be burned or pinched.

Bug Screen

In very cold weather the shutters may not keep enough heat in to warm the engine. Then a canvas, plastic, or leather screen can replace the bug screen. This is called a WINTER BLANKET.

Winter Blanket

Truck bumpers are made of different materials and in different shapes. Steel or aluminum is used for a FULL-WIDTH BUMPER that runs the entire width of the cab. The same materials are used for the CHOP BUMPER. The chop bumper is cut at both ends so it won't rub the tires in the event it is bent. It also is lighter than the full-width bumper.

Full-Width Bumper   Chop Bumper

When a trailer is not being used, it is placed on two DOLLY LEGS (supports). These legs prop the front part of the trailer up so the tractor can be backed easily under it. The legs are raised when the trailer is moving so they won't hit the ground.

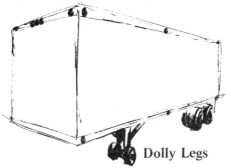

Dolly Legs

The DOLLY WHEELS on the bottom of the legs carry a lot of weight (psi—pounds per square inch). This weight often causes them to sink into the pavement, so a SAND SHOE can be used to replace the dolly wheel. With a sand shoe, the weight is spread over a larger area, and the dolly leg does not damage the pavement.

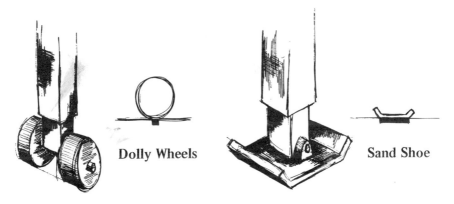

Dolly Wheels

Sand Shoe

57

The RUNNING GEAR (or suspension) of a tractor, trailer, or truck must be cushioned to provide a smooth ride. Usually the running gear is cushioned by a SPRING-SUSPENSION SYSTEM.

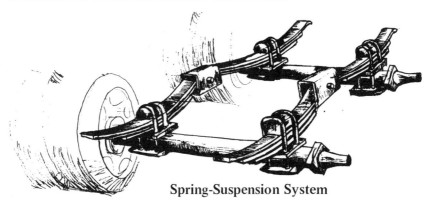

Spring-Suspension System

The shape of a truck's cab is determined by the type of load the truck will carry. The LONG-NOSE CONVENTIONAL CAB, with the engine in front of

Long-Nose Conventional Cab

the driver, gives a better ride for both driver and cargo.

Short-Nose
Conventional Cab

When very long trailers are being moved, the SHORT-NOSE CONVENTIONAL CAB is used. Most of the engine is in front of the driver but part of it extends under the cab so more length can be given to the trailer.

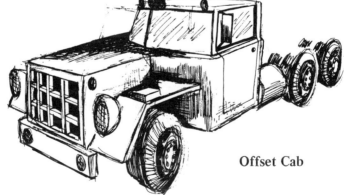

Offset Cab

The OFFSET CAB is a combination of the

conventional and the C.O.E. types. The cab is smaller and the engine extends beside it.

A LIFTGATE is like an elevator. It is on the rear or side of a trailer. The liftgate, run by hydraulic or electric power, loads and unloads heavy cargo where there is no loading dock.

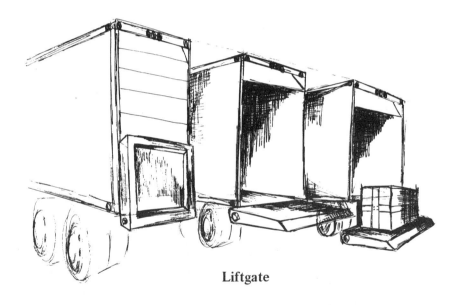

Liftgate

You may see a truck that has a plate, very much like a license plate, except that it is divided into small squares. This plate is called a RECIPROCITY PLATE. Various states issue reciprocity stickers, the size of postage stamps, that are placed in the squares on the plate. These stickers show that the truck has met the requirements of particular states.

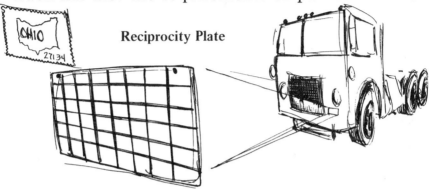

Reciprocity Plate

Tractors and trucks have air and electrical lines at the rear. AIR LINES operate the trailer brakes.

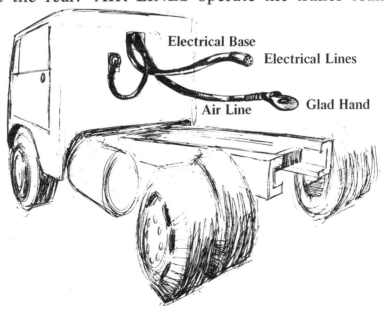

Electrical Base

Electrical Lines

Air Line

Glad Hand

At the end of the air line is a GLAD HAND that locks the lines together to prevent any loss of air. ELECTRICAL LINES operate the trailer lights. The ELECTRICAL BASE at the end of this line ensures proper wiring connections.

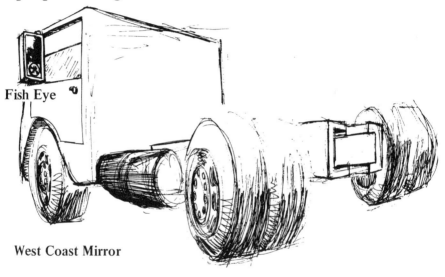

Fish Eye

West Coast Mirror

The large mirrors on the side of the tractor permit rear vision. They are called WEST COAST MIRRORS. They are often heated by electrical current to keep them clear of ice or snow. A spot mirror, or FISH EYE, is attached to the West Coast mirror to give the driver a complete view to the side and rear.

The driver's seat is often cushioned by an air bag.
This AIR-RIDE SEAT makes the ride much
smoother.

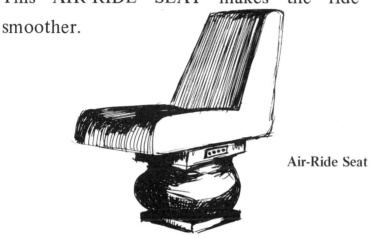

Air-Ride Seat

Some trailers are equipped with lift pads along the
sides that allow a crane to lift the trailer onto rail

Piggyback Van

cars. This type of trailer, called a PIGGYBACK or PIG VAN, also has four locking bars on the rear doors and extra vertical posts to give it added strength while being lifted or lowered.

Now that you have finished this book about the different types of trucks and their equipment, you will be able to spot so many new features whenever you see a truck. You may even want to make a game of it with your brother, sister, or friend. See who can identify types of trucks and parts of trucks first. Good luck, and keep on truckin'!

INDEX

DATE DUE

MAY 7			

HIGHSMITH 45-102   PRINTED IN U.S.A.